HOW THEY LIVE

EAGLES

JOHN ANDREWS

Brian Trodd Publishing House Limited

A White-tailed or Sea
Eagle *(Haliaeetus
albicilla)*.

Contents

Eagles and Other Birds of Prey

Eagles are large, broad-winged birds of prey. In the popular imagination they are strong, fierce birds with a high degree of hunting skill. They live in remote, wild country, and have a romantic aura about them. Nor are ornithologists, amateur and professional alike, immune to their mystique: eagles are special and simply seeing one is a major excitement and pleasure. However, there is a different but equally strong reaction from many shepherds, peasant farmers and gamekeepers who regard eagles as pests – killers of lambs, poultry or game – to be killed in turn by fair means or foul. Right or wrong, each side holds passionately to its view.

Rather surprisingly, there is in fact no exact definition of an eagle. The name is applied to a very wide range of birds of prey. Some are very large indeed, some are relatively small, some feed on monkeys, others on fish, snakes or rodents. Their habitats range from sub-arctic conditions to tropical rain forest. Indeed, while all authorities would agree that certain birds are eagles, they would argue about others, so it is necessary to start by reviewing their position relative to other hunting birds.

Two major groups of "raptors" have evolved. One is the owls, and the other we

Flying all out and calling loudly, an American Bald Eagle shows very clearly the strength and size so characteristic of all eagles.

call simply "birds of prey". Owls belong to the order *Strigiformes* and birds of prey to the order *Falconiformes*. They are unrelated but have certain physical characteristics in common, such as taloned feet and hooked beaks, because they have developed some similarities in their lifestyles. The order *Falconiformes* divides into three suborders, the members of each having some features uniquely in common. The first suborder is the *Cathartae*, or New World vultures. The second is the *Accipitres* which includes all the eagles as well as the Old World vultures, kites, harriers, buzzards and many other species. The third is the *Falcones*, effectively comprising the falcons of the world – mostly high-speed interceptors of flying prey.

The *Accipitres* are divided into two superfamilies, the Secretary Bird (*Sagittarius serpentarius*) being the sole and surprising member of one of these, while the other superfamily – the *Accipitroidea* is divided into two families, one of which contains only the Osprey (*Pandion haliaeetus*), while the other family, the *Accipitridae*, contains over 200 species grouped in turn into subfamilies. All the birds considered as eagles are in the family *Accipitridae* but they are not necessarily very closely related to each other.

The subfamily *Haliaeetinae* contains three different genera, totalling 11 species

Above: One of the strangest of all birds of prey, the Secretary bird kills snakes by stamping on them.

Left: While eagles are the largest of the day-flying raptors, they have their equivalent among the night hunters. The Great Horned Owl is capable of killing small deer and wolf cubs.

all known as sea eagles or fish eagles. As their names imply, these birds specialize in hunting in aquatic habitats, both marine and fresh water. This requires specialized techniques for detecting and catching fish, but the birds also take waterfowl, amphibians and, in some species, a wide range of other prey and carrion. Indeed many eagles are opportunist hunters and feeders, taking both live and dead prey.

The subfamily *Circaetinae* contains five genera of snake or serpent eagles, 12 species in all. As their name implies, snakes are an important source of food. These eagles take both poisonous and non-poisonous snakes, relying primarily on their efficient killing skills to protect themselves because, though their thick-skinned legs and body feathers provide some physical protection, they are not immune to snake venom. Most of these

Lakes, rivers and the sea are rich hunting grounds, stocked with fish and waterfowl. Several species of eagle, including the African Fish Eagle, have evolved the skills to capture prey from the water's surface.

species also take reptiles, rodents and other prey. One of them, the Bateleur (*Terathopius ecaudatus*), takes some snakes including the highly venomous Puff Adder (and has indeed been killed by it) but its main food is mammals and birds. It also takes much carrion and is, or was, renowned among the Zulus for feeding on human corpses after battles.

The subfamily *Buteoninae* contains 14 genera including the buzzards. It is debatable whether the four species of so-called buzzard-eagles merit the name but there can be no question about the two species of solitary eagles *(Harpyhaliaeetus)*, the Guyana Crested Eagle (*Morphnus guianensis*), the Harpy *(Harpia harpyja)*, the New Guinea Harpy (*Harpyopsis novaeguineae*) or the Philippine Eagle (*Pithecophaga jefferyi*), all of which are predators of arboreal mammals such as monkeys and sloths as well as birds.

Right: Often eagles mantle their newly-captured prey with their wings – clearly signalling to other birds that the meal is not to be shared. Small prey, such as this Water Monitor Lizard taken by an immature Martial Eagle, will probably be consumed at one sitting.

Below: The African Crowned Eagle also ranks among the most powerful birds of prey. Here, with crest erect and wings half spread, an adult threatens an interloper. Actual physical conflict is rarely necessary!

With the subfamily *Aquilinae* we come to eight genera with 20 species all of which are regarded as eagles. They include what is arguably the most powerful of all birds, the Crowned Eagle (*Stephanoaetus coronatus*), which can kill an antelope up to four times its own weight and is reliably documented as attempting to carry off a seven-year-old African boy. The genus *Aquila* contains what most ornithologists regard as *the* eagles including the Golden (*A. chrysaetos*), Imperial (*A. heliaca*) and Tawny Eagle (*A. rapax*). By contrast the genus *Hieraaetus* includes some of the smaller species including the Booted Eagle (*H. pennatus*) which, with a wingspan of 1–1.2m (3ft 3in–3ft 9in) is slightly smaller and slimmer than a Common Buzzard (*Buteo buteo*).

So there is in fact no precise cut-off point from other birds of prey in terms of size, food, or shape. However, it is clear that, in general, eagles are bigger than other species, and their size is very significant in affecting the way they live. All

living creatures are in competition with at least some other species for food. They reduce the competition by specializing – taking only one kind of food perhaps, or developing a special way of gathering it. Birds of prey have become flesh-eaters; vultures, for example, specialize in carrion, while eagles take some carrion but mostly take live prey and generally kill rather large animals. Different subfamilies of eagle tend to specialize in different types of prey – fish, reptiles or monkeys for instance – and, within a subfamily, different species live in different places to reduce competition even further.

Dependence on large prey may have some advantages; the bigger the animal you can overpower, the less often you may need to hunt, for instance. But it also has disadvantages, because bigger prey itself tends to be scarcer than smaller animals as it needs more food – grass, fruit, insects or whatever. This means that eagles need large hunting ranges to hold enough food to support themselves, and therefore cannot ever be very numerous. Small changes in their environment can drastically affect

their food supply and this in turn may have very serious effects on them.

But there are many compensatory advantages of size. Being big enables any creature to go far longer without food, partly because it can store more fat and partly because larger animals lose heat, and so burn up their energy reserves, relatively more slowly than small ones. So short-term food shortages may simply mean that the eagle sits it out, hunched motionless in a tree or on a crag until conditions improve.

Large creatures also tend to be long-lived. Although mortality of young eagles is quite high until they have fully developed their hunting skills, once maturity is reached the bird can expect ten or 20 years of life. This means that the rate of reproduction can be very low since a pair of adults only needs to have two offspring survive to adulthood to maintain the population. If poor conditions mean that the birds cannot breed, or fail in the attempt, there is usually another chance. Some birds of prey, because they are long-lived, invest a lot of effort in rearing their young, caring for them for long periods after they have left the nest so as to maximize their chances of survival.

An adult Bald Eagle returns to its chicks. Eagles must invest much energy in rearing their young and helping them to learn to hunt successfully.

The primary or flight
feathers of an eagle
are particularly
noticeable, and provide
the bird with the
ability to travel at
speed and cope with
strong air currents.

How Eagles Fly

To survive, eagles have to be superb flyers. Most of the creatures that they hunt are wary, and quick to react to danger by diving into cover, by agile evasion or by relying on their own speed to escape. Few prey animals are defenceless, having teeth or poisoned fangs, claws or hooves, and the ability to use them effectively. Injury is often fatal to creatures which hunt, as even a slight impairment of hunting ability may reduce the success rate or increase the likelihood of another injury. Either way, there is a risk of death, either directly, or indirectly as a result of starvation. This means that an eagle must be able to approach its prey so rapidly that it is taken by surprise or overhauled and captured after only a brief chase, and the apparent ease with which eagles and other predators kill their prey reflects the stark fact that if they are not highly efficient they are soon dead themselves!

When the eagle has caught and killed its prey, the bird must be able to lift it from the ground and carry it to a safe place to be eaten. Otherwise it runs the risk of being robbed by other hunters, including larger birds of prey and terrestrial predators such as wolves or hyaenas. When there are young in the nest, the eagle may have to carry food back to them from a long distance.

Some species live in mountainous or sub-arctic country where there are often long periods of continuous high wind and storms of rain or snow. Although all eagles can go for days without feeding, obviously there comes a time when the bird must hunt or starve, so the ability to fly in the worst weather is essential.

Down the long ages all sorts of creatures have evolved the ability to glide or fly – pterodactyls and bats, some kinds of fish, and many insects as well as birds. But birds' mastery of flight lies in the amazing properties of their most special possession – feathers.

In mountainous country, eagles may have to cope with long periods of rain or snow when hunting is difficult.

A flight feather has to form a fairly flat and continuous surface so that air can flow over it. Each feather consists of a central shaft with great numbers of barbs (**c**) on each side. Alongside the upper and lower edges are barbules (**a**) which lock together with hooks (**b**).

Feathers are made of *keratin*, the same material as hair, horns, hooves, beaks and claws and all the other hard external parts of mammals and birds. They are rather complicated things. Each consists of a central shaft with great numbers of branches (called *barbs*) lying close against each other up each side. These barbs have rows of tiny hooks (called *barbules*) along their upper and lower edges so that they all lock together, rather like a series of zip fasteners. The whole feather forms a fairly flat surface which is very flexible and surprisingly strong. Its precise shape depends on the function it is required to fulfil.

The flexible flight feathers at the end of a bird's wing. Almost all the barbs are on one side of the central shaft.

The feathers at the end of a bird's wing are called the *primaries* or flight feathers. Each of these is long and flexible, usually with almost all the barbs forming a "vane" on one side of the shaft only. If you hold a primary feather firmly and move it sharply downwards you will see that, as it presses against the air, the end first twists and then, as it reaches a point where its structural resistance prevents further twisting, the angled part is forced forward by the air's resistance. With a large feather like an eagle's, you can feel this propulsion power quite clearly. At this stage, the feather is functioning in the same way as the propeller on an aircraft, so that when all the primaries of both wings are forced down through the air, the whole bird is pushed forwards. Depending on the rate at which the wings are beaten, and the depth of the stroke, the force and duration of each propulsive stroke can be varied, to alter overall speed.

In small birds, the primary feathers are not particularly noticeable but in eagles they are usually very obvious, sticking out like separate fingers at the end of the wing and providing the bird with the ability to travel at great speed and to cope with strong air currents, though only for a limited time.

However, in order to fly, birds need lift as well as forward propulsion. Lift comes from the shape of the wing. It is difficult to see this in flight but if you can look at the wing of a dead bird you will find that the upper surface is slightly arched from front to back and that the underside is flat or even slightly hollow. The wings of an aircraft also have this special form, called an *aerofoil*. In cross section, the wing is not flat but curved. The important thing is that the upper surface is more curved than the lower one. This means that the distance from the front edge of the wing to the back is longer over the top than it is underneath. This makes air travel faster over the top of the wing than under it which makes a slight difference in air pressure because, in effect, the air above the wing is "stretched" and becomes thinner than the air underneath. The result is that the pressure from the denser air underneath pushes the wing upwards keeping the bird aloft.

Because birds can alter the angle of their wings, and the total area of the wing surface by opening and closing it, they can alter the amount of lift that they get from the aerofoil, and so climb or descend at an angle or use the wings as brakes.

Juvenile birds, like this young Bald Eagle, run a high risk of injury or starvation until they become skilled in capturing and killing their prey.

The Australian Wedge-tailed Eagle is one of several species with rather long tails, which aid them in steering rapidly through woodland or scrub.

The eagle's tail is important for steering. Species like the Harpy, which hunt through cover, and must be highly manoeuvrable, have relatively long tails, whereas fish eagles, operating in open conditions, have short or wedge-shaped tails. The Bateleur has the shortest tail of all. It steers its way at high speed across grassland or through the well-spaced trees of the bushveld by canting its wings – hence its name, which means balancer or tightrope-walker, and was given to it by the French naturalist Le Vaillant.

When the bird thumps down on its prey, it must be able to stop almost instantly or risk being damaged itself in the crash. The spread wings and tail make a para-

chute shape that decelerates the bird very efficiently. Much of the remaining shock of impact is deliberately transferred to the prey as the feet are thrown forward to strike and grasp, winding the victim or knocking it to the ground.

Although the most important thing about feathers is that they make it possible for birds to fly and for eagles, in particular, to fly high and range far in pursuit of their prey, feathers have other uses too.

The body of an eagle, like any other bird, is clothed in an overlapping coat of slightly curved oval feathers – rather like tiles on a roof – which are called *contour feathers* because they follow the contours

The Bateleur steers by tilting its wings and body, and is almost tailless. This bird has captured a large lizard.

Feathers readily shed water, and so several eagles have taken to fishing. This Bald Eagle illustrates the classic movement of attack – feet forward to grasp the prey, wings spread to control speed, and head pulled back out of harm's way.

of the bird's body. They are important for two reasons. One is to protect the bird from injury if it hits a branch when landing or taking off, or if its prey fights back before it is overpowered and killed. The other important functions of contour feathers are to insulate the body from extremes of temperature and to keep it dry. Provided the feathers are clean, moisture cannot stick to them. So, when a Philippine Eagle is caught in a tropical downpour or an African Fish Eagle *(Haliaeetus vocifer)* has splashed into the surface of a lake to capture a big catfish, the water will immediately run off its close-fitting coat.

The hunter and the hunted: a Golden Eagle prepares to strike its prey. Its victim has no hope of escaping such a powerful attack.

17

Their large size helps eagles to cope with cold conditions. Two adult and two immature Bald Eagles relax in sub-zero conditions in the mountains of Alaska.

Between their contour feathers and skin, eagles, like other birds, have a layer of down. Down is simply feathers without barbules on the barbs, so that it forms a fluffy layer which traps the air and prevents both loss of heat outwards in winter and absorption of heat inwards in summer.

Some species of eagle routinely cope with extremes of temperature which other creatures, including Man, cannot readily tolerate. For instance, Golden Eagles in Scotland stay on their territories year round, living through several months of snow and high winds, when the chill factor becomes dangerous. Their size helps them cope with cold because the ratio of surface area to body volume is less than in a smaller bird, so that heat loss is less. They are also careful in choice of roost sites, seeking locations with minimal exposure to wind.

As well as working very well to protect birds from temperature variations, down has another quality – it is very lightweight. This is most important because the more weight the bird has to lift when flying, the more energy it uses up. Some of the larger eagles are close to the weight limit for bird flight and additional weight is simply not an option.

In the rough and tumble of daily use, feathers get damaged. Often the barbules come unzipped. So eagles spend a good deal of time preening themselves, running each feather carefully through the beak in order to zip it up again and keep it clean.

Despite preening, feathers eventually become worn. Then old feathers are moulted and new ones grow to replace them. Loss of flight feathers can impair mobility. Some birds, notably waterfowl, lose all their primaries at once and are briefly flightless but they can choose sites where food is abundant, and avoid pre-dators by swimming and diving. Eagles have no such option; a flightless eagle will starve if it is not first killed and eaten by another predator. So the birds lose only one primary feather from each wing at a time, which means that their propulsion is only slightly reduced. You can often see gaps in the wings or tail feathers of large birds of prey when they pass overhead.

Gliding and soaring use little energy but depend on suitable wind conditions or warm-air thermals.

Flight takes a lot of muscle power. Down the centre of a bird's chest, the *sternum* or breastbone sticks out like a keel to which are anchored the powerful muscles whose other ends are attached to the bones of the wings. Obviously, if you have strong muscles pulling between two sets of bones, and bones propelling wing feathers against air resistance, the bones themselves must be strong enough to take the strain. One evolutionary challenge for birds has been to develop bones which have adequate strength with minimum weight, so as to reduce the energy demands of flight. Birds have solved this by evolving bones with an interior structure like honeycomb – lots of small hollow cells separated by struts of bony material running from side to side. This provides excellent stress resistance.

For the wing muscles to work efficiently they have to receive a good supply of oxygen. They also have to be cooled or the eagle would overheat. Operating at high altitudes – and many eagles fly so high they are invisible from the ground – they face, like mountaineers, the problem of oxygen shortage. To solve this the circulatory and respiratory systems of birds are different from those of mammals, providing a larger surface area for the absorption of oxygen by the blood, and enabling air to circulate further inside the body cavity.

Powered flapping flight also uses up energy and this is important because the more energy a bird uses the more prey it must catch. If the bird can save energy in some way then it needs to catch less food to survive or to breed successfully. That enables it to expand into places where prey is scarce and where, perhaps, there is little or no competition from other predators, and it is better able to survive hard times when food is scarce, as in the winter. Eagles and other large birds of prey, notably vultures and buzzards, have developed a means of flying which actually saves energy and so gives them these benefits.

When the sun rises and warms the ground, heat is transferred to the adjoining air and the warm air itself begins to rise just as it will from a fire or a radiator.

This rising current or bubble of warm air, called a *thermal*, can quickly develop considerable lifting power. Obviously it will work best when it is pushing against a large surface capable of capturing a lot of the power, and this is why these birds have such long, broad wings. Spreading them out stiffly, they can soar on the thermal without flapping. To stay within the rising thermal they glide in circles and so are lifted effortlessly until the gradually cooling air ceases to be effective.

A Bald Eagle soars high above the wilds of Alaska.

Rising air currents also occur where the wind strikes a hill or mountainside and is forced upwards over the slope. This can create a wave of moving air passing over the top of a hill, and a large bird of prey can easily soar to and fro along it. This helps the birds to live in mountainous areas which get little sunshine in winter.

In general, eagles and other soaring birds of prey such as buzzards and vultures are late risers. They simply sit around until the sun has warmed the ground sufficiently to produce strong thermals. Then they can glide out from their roosts and rise easily into the sky to a height from which they can travel across country by gliding stiff-winged, slowly losing height, until they find another thermal. Now the bird can soar up again, perhaps until it is almost invisible from the ground. Gliding and soaring by turns, the bird can quickly travel far across country with almost no effort at all. Probably the birds learn to recognize physical landforms likely to create thermals and prefer to glide towards places where the chance of finding a thermal is greatest.

Though among the smallest birds of prey which can be considered as eagles, the Black-chested Buzzard Eagle has very broad wings and a short, wide tail which together form a flying shape that is ideal for gliding at low speed.

their energy demands and perhaps failing to catch anything.

As it happens, sitting still is not a bad way of hunting, and some eagles habitually employ it as a technique. Mammals and birds may come close, unaware of the lurking danger, and easily fall victim.

But hunting is never easy, even for eagles. The creatures on which they prey are all cautious about coming into the open. Many are camouflaged and are difficult to see. They keep a constant lookout for any threat. They are quick to take flight, to run or dive for cover when danger threatens. If they live in groups, as do grouse, geese and rabbits, then there is almost always one individual on watch while others feed. Some animals, such as meerkats, actually post sentries whose sole duty is to watch out for predators. The hunting eagle must therefore see its potential prey before it is seen, plan its approach to maximize the element of surprise, and finally achieve a clean, quick kill.

Left: African Martial Eagles spend long hours perched, but are always watchful for unwary prey.

Below: As a protection against predators including eagles, Meerkats have developed a complex social system in which all take turns to stand up on guard.

But, as with every other aspect of evolutionary adaptation, every advantage has its disadvantage. The large wing size ideal for exploiting thermals needs great amounts of muscle-power and energy to work when thermals are not available. So, when conditions are totally unsuitable for flying, as in cold, rainy or still weather, most eagles will simply not bother to fly at all. Under normal circumstances they have considerable stores of body fat which can be easily metabolized for nutrition and warmth, and it is less risky to stay put and draw on these resources than to set off on a flight where they will have to flap for long periods, greatly increasing

The Supreme Hunter

Keen eyesight is essential. All eagles have very large eyes. They are sometimes brown but often red, orange or yellow, which can give the bird a rather wild expression. But do not be misled. Those eyes are much more efficient than ours, and can spot a rabbit feeding in a field two or three times as far away as we can.

Birds' eyes work in much the same way as ours do. Light enters through the pupil and strikes a screen at the back of the eye, called the retina. This sheet of cells records an image and passes the "picture" on to the brain. There are two sorts of light-sensitive cells – *rods*, which are very important to creatures which operate in poor light or darkness, like owls or cats, and *cones*, which are important for the sharpness of the picture and colour vision. Eagles have retinas rich in cone cells so that they produce a much sharper colour picture of even distant, tiny objects than any human eye can do.

Of course, many of the creatures on which eagles prey have quite good eyesight themselves. But they are at a disadvantage because they must keep a lookout in all directions at once, since they cannot predict where danger lies. It is no good for them to have eyesight which can

Relative to head size, eagles' eyes are much larger than that of humans, but they share with us the forward binocular gaze of hunters. This is the snake-eating Short-toed Eagle.

pinpoint a distant predator in one direction if, while they are watching it, another enemy may be approaching from the other side or from behind. And of course, many prey animals are not solely hunted by eagles. They must watch out not only for birds in the air but also for danger from foxes, stoats and wild cats, for example. They achieve all-round vision by having their eyes set on each side of the head so that they can look in both directions at once and, at the same time, see right across the sky from one horizon to the other when standing erect.

However, no prey animal can spend all its life on guard. A lot of time has to be spent feeding, and in spring and summer they must find mates and rear families. The skilled hunter picks the time when its prey is not paying proper attention to the danger from the skies. When it is busily feeding or otherwise occupied, the hunting bird has the best chance of getting really close before it is spotted. When eagles are young and first learning to hunt for themselves they make silly mistakes, trying to capture animals which are on their guard. As a result, they often fail to catch anything, or are injured, and mortality in young eagles is high.

Because they are predators, eagles' eyes are not placed on the sides of their heads for all-round vision but face forwards so that they can focus on their prey with both eyes at once. In this way they can judge distance when they are really close to the prey and about to grasp it in their talons.

Eagles have several different strategies for hunting and some species use different methods depending on the type of habitat, the likely prey or even the weather.

Most prey animals, such as this Cottontail Rabbit, have bulging eyes set on the sides of the head to give nearly complete all-round vision.

A Martial Eagle prepares for take-off. The pose reveals the very long legs typical of many species of eagle – an important aid to capturing fleeing prey and for holding it safely "at arms' length".

One approach is simply to sit still and wait until prey comes into view. By doing this the eagle is using hardly any energy, which means that it does not need to catch so much in order to "refuel". And sitting still has another advantage. The eagle is even less likely to be spotted by the prey before it has had time to plan and launch an attack.

But where prey is scarce then the eagle must set out to search. This is where the ability to soar is immensely valuable. Once the eagle can find an upcurrent it can go up so high that it is invisible from the ground but, with its own keen eyesight, it can still easily see everything that moves over a huge area. And because soaring takes up very little energy, the bird can wheel on stiff wings for hours, or glide from place to place, waiting for the ideal opportunity to come along.

Once the eagle spots its prey, it must carefully plan its attack. It would be no use simply swooping down, because long before it came close the prey would have taken flight and fled into cover. Instead, the big bird must approach as close as possible without being seen and this may even involve setting off at first in completely the opposite direction. What the eagle is doing is to make use of cover to hide its approach. For instance, it may fly right around the back of a hill to a place where it can lose height without being spotted and then, by flying much closer to the ground, remain invisible to its prey until it suddenly appears only a few yards away, perhaps swooping down over the top of some nearby trees or appearing as if by magic out of a fold in the ground. An African Martial Eagle (*Polemaetus bellicosus*) was once seen to start its attack

Although flapping flight uses up energy, this Golden Eagle's low-altitude approach may enable it to get close to its victims unobserved.

27

with a long, shallow descent starting 6km (4 miles) away from its intended victim.

However, although soaring gives the eagle an ability to search easily over very large areas, it does not solve the problem of hunting where there are plenty of trees or scrub to provide cover. Here, the only solution may be to fly steadily through the trees and come upon prey completely unawares. Then it is a case of grabbing the victim before it has time to flee or fight. Eagles like the Harpy, which normally hunt inside forests, have shorter, broader wings than those which hunt in open country and longer tails for better steering control. This makes it easier for them to weave between the branches.

Some eagles have chosen to hunt creatures whose eyesight is much less powerful than, for instance, that of a hare or pheasant. But such prey have, of course, other defences. Snakes for instance are first of all very hard to see. Coiled up and basking motionless in the sun, they are easy to overlook. To search for them, the Short-toed Eagle (*Circaetus gallicus*) will hover no more than 15m (50ft) above the ground, flapping its wings laboriously in order to peer carefully in every likely spot. On spotting a snake it drops like a stone. But the snake still has two other defences. It can move like lightning, and when the eagle is at last seen – a dark, swiftly-falling shape against the sky – the snake will whisk into cover if it can. And many snakes are poisonous and may strike back at an eagle that fumbles the kill.

The eagle's weapons are its feet. It has strong, muscular legs and feet and is equipped with eight, needle-sharp talons. In the very last moment before it grasps its prey, the eagle throws its head and body backwards and its legs and feet forwards, so that it hits its victim feet-first. The speed and weight of the bird may well knock over a large prey so that it is immediately winded and struggling at a disadvantage.

Short-toed Eagles habitually fly low, gliding and hovering as they search for lizards and snakes.

As this Golden Eagle blinks, it shows the semi-transparent inner eyelid which is shut to protect the eye from damage when landing or capturing prey.

An eagle's feet are its killing tools. The toes are strong and are equipped with long, curved talons which are driven in like daggers.

Still holding its head well back out of harm's way, the eagle tightens its grip, driving the talons like so many daggers deep into the body of its victim. Death is often instantaneous, and one can hardly even call it cruel because the whole business lasts a few seconds at most. It may be that eagles deliberately seek to puncture a vital spot, penetrating the heart or severing the spinal cord.

If the victim does manage to fight back, the eagle is protected in several ways. Its legs and feet are covered by tough scales, which may be strong enough to resist the bite of a snake. The body feathers are strong and dense so that it is not easy to strike a blow that seriously damages the bird. The eagle's eyes are also protected by transparent skin, which it can wink across rather like safety goggles. All birds have this protective membrane, the *nictitating membrane*, and will flick it closed when landing amongst foliage or when fighting.

Once the prey is dead, the eagle may choose to eat it on the spot or carry it off to some place where it is in no danger of being robbed, by a big cat or a timber wolf perhaps. Large prey may be much too heavy to lift from the ground. It will be dismembered on the spot and the various parts stowed safely in trees out of the reach of such competitors. A large kill can provide a single eagle or a mated pair with enough food to last them several days, the birds returning to their larder at need. This is another advantage of being able to kill large prey, because the birds need expend little energy while the food lasts.

The eagle uses its beak to pluck the prey roughly, if it is a bird, or to tear open the skin of a mammal or snake. Then the hooked upper beak is driven into the flesh, the two halves of the beak are closed like a pair of pliers and the eagle tugs off a bite-sized chunk of meat, gulping it down whole or feeding it, with surprising care and delicacy, to its chicks.

An eagle can kill and eat practically anything smaller than itself. In different parts of the world they take wolf cubs, foxes, deer, large game birds, other birds of prey, fish, snakes and lizards, frogs and toads, small songbirds, mice and even beetles. Some can kill much bigger creatures too. The African Crowned Eagle can overpower antelopes four to six times its own weight. Although it is not as large as some other African eagles it has exceptionally large and powerful feet – the hind

Eagles are so efficient they can often kill creatures larger than themselves. Here a Martial Eagle starts to feed on an antelope.

31

Black Eagles feed almost entirely on Rock Hyraxes, which weigh half as much again as the birds themselves.

claw is as thick as a man's little finger.

Some species normally specialize in what they kill. The Black Eagle, also called Verraux's Eagle (*Aquila verrauxi*), lives in mountainous country in Africa and almost all its food consists of Rock Hyraxes, or dassies. These animals weigh about 4kg (9lb), whereas the eagle weighs only 3kg (6½lb), and it has been calculated that a pair of Black Eagles and their single offspring account for about 400 hyrax a year. Even so, they are opportunist feeders. They will rob other birds – one was seen to attack a vulture, forcing it to drop a piece of carrion which the eagle

then caught in the air and carried off. Black Eagles also feed on locusts, picking them from the ground at times when they are swarming and so abundant that they are easy to catch in large quantities.

Some eagles take a good deal of carrion. The Tawny Eagle sometimes feeds with vultures, but some individuals are very aggressive and one was observed to keep 20 vultures off the carcass on which it wished to feed. In the past this eagle would frequent native villages to scavenge offal, and used to be recorded as accompanying shoots to snatch and carry off wounded birds!

Despite their strength and formidable weapons, many young eagles die before they are two years old. Usually, the youngsters wander away from where they were born, looking for a place of their own where prey is plentiful. But most of the good areas are already occupied by other eagles which tolerate no competition and drive the young bird away. It may be forced to hunt in places where food is scarce or hard to capture. Only the strongest and cleverest individuals survive.

Sometimes the young bird is lucky, and is accepted by an adult eagle whose mate has died. But it may have to wander far, and wait for years, before it finally wins itself a territory. Not until an eagle is four or five years old is it a sufficiently skilled hunter to try to rear a family.

Confusingly, this species has two populations with distinct lifestyles. One, known as the Tawny Eagle and seen here, is resident in Africa and often feeds on carrion. The other is known as the Steppe Eagle: it breeds in central Asia and winters in Africa.

Competition for territories and food is often intense. Even Bald Eagles, which can occur in large numbers where food is abundant, will squabble over prey and breeding sites.

33

Breeding and Rearing the Young

At the start of the breeding season the male must display, both to discourage other males from attempting to move into its territory, and to encourage a female to mate with him.

Some eagles hold huge territories. In Africa, pairs of Martial Eagle nest 30 or 40km (12–19 miles) apart and this is probably because they need this size of hunting range. Obviously, if eagles deplete the numbers of prey as a result of their hunting, they make conditions more difficult for themselves. They can only safely harvest a surplus, and kill no more animals than can be replaced by breeding. No eagle can specialize in prey that breeds only slowly. There is of course no conscious decision-making about this. As the population of a particular creature is reduced, it becomes harder to find, and so the eagles are likely to switch to other more abundant species. This then allows the depleted stock an opportunity to recover. It is the abundance of prey which controls the number of eagles, and if prey declines due to breeding failure or habitat

The flying signature of a Black Eagle, signalling to other eagles that it has laid claim to a territory.

change the eagles suffer in consequence.

Defending a large territory requires special techniques, and eagles generally rely on aerial advertising, flying up high so as to be seen from far off. Some eagles make stupendous dives from hundreds of feet. Others dive and fall in a switchback pattern across the sky. This flying signature is quickly recognized by other eagles of the same species.

Such aerial displays are unnecessary for eagles which nest close together. African Fish Eagles sometimes nest only a few hundred metres apart when fish are abundant and easy to catch. They display mainly by calling loudly, though they have a splendid courtship dance, in which male and female lock their feet together and whirl over and over through the air.

In his courtship of the female, a male eagle may bring her gifts of freshly killed food. This extra food helps her to make the eggs and gives her reserves of fat to live on during the long period of incubation, when she cannot hunt for herself.

Before egg laying, a nest must be built. Some eagles use the same nest sites every year. It makes sense to stick to places which have proved to be safe. Golden Eagles may have two or three preferred sites within a territory and the one they use in any particular year may depend on how fast winter snow clears. If the best site is still under snow when the birds need to start breeding they will take the second choice.

Breeding cannot be delayed. It is critically important that prey is abundant when the young bird leaves the nest and first has to fend for itself, so the start of breeding is timed to ensure this. An early start is usually essential, even before the last snowfalls, so that the female Golden Eagle may actually be successfully incubating her eggs with snow settling on her back!

Eagle nests are very big, made of sticks up to a metre long, so they do not rot down

quickly or blow away. Often this means that the remains of the nest are still there when the birds come back in the following year. They build the new nest on top of the old one and, eventually, the pile can become quite massive – 3m (9ft 9in) across and 5m (16ft) high in the case of some American Bald Eagles (*Haliaeetus leucocephalus*).

Nest construction is a long job. It can take a pair of African Crowned Eagles four or five months to build a completely new nest, and a month or longer to repair and line an existing one so that it is suitable for egg laying. The birds get new material by bouncing up and down on tree branches until they snap off! When the main structure is complete, the nest cup is lined with green foliage.

The impressive aerial courtship of African Fish Eagles who whirl over and over in the air, feet interlocked.

Sites where the adults are successful in rearing young will often be used again and again over the years. The nests then become very large as more material is added each season.

Generally, the larger eagles lay only one egg and smaller species have two or three. This may suggest that the biggest birds, having the greatest energy demands, actually find it harder to rear young than their smaller relations do.

Most kinds of eagle lay two eggs, though some have one or three. As soon as the first egg is laid, the female starts to incubate, snuggling it up inside her breast feathers so that it is kept warm by her body heat.

It may take nearly two months before the eggs hatch. For most of that time, the female will be sitting patiently on the nest and the male will bring food to her every few days. If hunting is poor, she may go for up to two weeks without food. Occasionally, the male may relieve her at the nest so that she can go off to hunt for herself, but often females become reluctant to desert their task even briefly and the male may have gently to push his mate away to get her to let him take a turn.

Growth of a chick inside the egg begins

from the time when the female starts to incubate it. Most birds wait until the clutch is complete before starting incubation, but eagles incubate from the first egg which therefore hatches slightly before the second one.

The chick gets its first feed soon after it hatches, and grows so quickly that it is quite a bit larger than the second chick when this hatches in turn. In most species of eagle, the larger chick then usually either bullies the smaller one so that it obtains no food and eventually starves, or actually attacks and kills it.

Strangely, the parents make no move to interfere and the reason for this behaviour is not understood. If one chick gets all the food then it can obviously grow faster which means that it is more likely to survive, but that does not explain why the female should lay two or three eggs in the first place, and then make no effort to protect her smaller young even when food is abundant.

Although she ignores the struggle between the chicks, the female is extremely

One of the greatest mysteries of eagle biology is why many species which lay more than one egg allow the oldest chick to kill its siblings.

gentle in feeding and caring for them, breaking up the prey which the male brings into small morsels which she holds out in her beak for a chick to take. When the weather is cold or wet, then one parent will brood it. If the sun is too hot, an adult will stand at the edge of the nest and shade the chick with half-spread wings, though it may be panting itself in the savage heat.

The adults also try to protect the young from predators and may swoop at animals or humans many times larger than themselves, even striking out with their talons. One American Bald Eagle was seen to try to chase off helicopters which came within a mile of the nest! Bateleur seem to use a distraction display, perching nearby and calling loudly, perhaps in an attempt to draw attention away from vulnerable eggs or offspring.

If the intruder does get to the nest, then the chick may throw itself on its back, presenting its big taloned feet to the danger in a courageous last attempt to defend itself.

If all goes well, the young eagle grows rapidly, replacing its down with proper adult feathers and, as its wings develop, exercising vigorously by standing on the edge of the nest and flapping hard. It takes young Golden Eagles more than two months from hatching to be ready to launch out into the world. Young African Black Eagles take three months.

When the young eagle leaves the nest, it has no idea how to hunt properly and would quickly starve if its parents did not continue to feed it. African Crowned Eagles continue to feed their chick for nearly a year after it leaves the nest, gradually reducing their support as the youngster learns the skills of hunting. Although this means that they can breed only every other year at most, it is obviously better to increase the survival chances of fewer young than to produce more and have them all die.

Opposite: The eaglet hatches with a dense coat of white down which helps to keep it warm. While it is still small, the female will shelter it from rain and cold, or from hot sunshine.

Left: Almost ready to leave the nest, this young Golden Eagle spends much time exercising its wings by flapping vigorously. It will be several years before it loses the white patches of plumage which identify it as a youngster.

Migrations

A full-grown eagle is well able to take care of itself. It can fly in high winds when most other birds are grounded. Some kinds live in country where the temperatures are below freezing for months at a time. Others, like the Philippine Eagle, live in humid tropical forests. But while eagles themselves can cope with all sorts of weather, the creatures they prey on may not be able to do so. If their prey hibernates or moves away during bad weather, then the eagles must follow their prey or face starvation.

The Short-toed Eagle, for example, spends the summer in southern Europe, feeding largely on snakes and other reptiles. In winter, snakes and lizards disappear, hibernating underground. So the Short-toed Eagles must migrate in the autumn to tropical Africa in order to find enough food to see them through the winter, only returning north in spring when the snakes and lizards have returned above ground, once more to bask in the sun.

Migration brings us back to another

Sitting on the ice these Bald Eagles may look thoroughly depressed, but they are well equipped to cope successfully with cold and with food shortage.

Dependent largely on reptiles which hibernate in winter, Short-toed Eagles must migrate south from Europe in autumn to pass the winter in Africa.

example of how evolutionary advantages also have drawbacks associated with them. The development of broad wings to enable eagles to soar on thermals and updraughts has made it impossible for them to undertake flapping flight for long periods of time. The muscles simply cannot power the huge wings except in fairly short bursts. This presents no problem over land but it makes it impossible for eagles to travel far over water.

The reason for this is quite simple. Water does not warm up quickly in the way that land does, so that rising thermals of warm air never occur over water. And when wind blows over water there is no obstruction to create an updraught. This means that an eagle crossing water would have to flap its wings continuously and would quickly become tired, sink to the surface and drown. So eagles never cross large bodies of water but go round the edge, soaring and gliding effortlessly from place to place.

In Europe this leads to concentrations of broad-winged birds of prey, mainly buzzards and eagles, at certain points where the geography of the land funnels them together. Migrants from Scandinavia "island hop" from Sweden to Denmark and birdwatchers visit Falsterbo to watch the birds moving through in autumn. Here there are few eagles with most of the migrants being Common Buzzards, Honey Buzzards (*Pernis apivorus*) and Sparrowhawks (*Accipiter nisus*). Moving south they are joined by other birds, some from Britain but many more from France, Germany, eastern and southern Europe. Now the migration divides, some birds swinging south-west towards Gibraltar and crossing the Straits to enter Africa, others heading south-east towards Turkey. Here they are squeezed between the Mediterranean and the Sea of Marmara on one side and the Black Sea on the other, so that they are forced to travel along the narrow "bridge" of land over

41

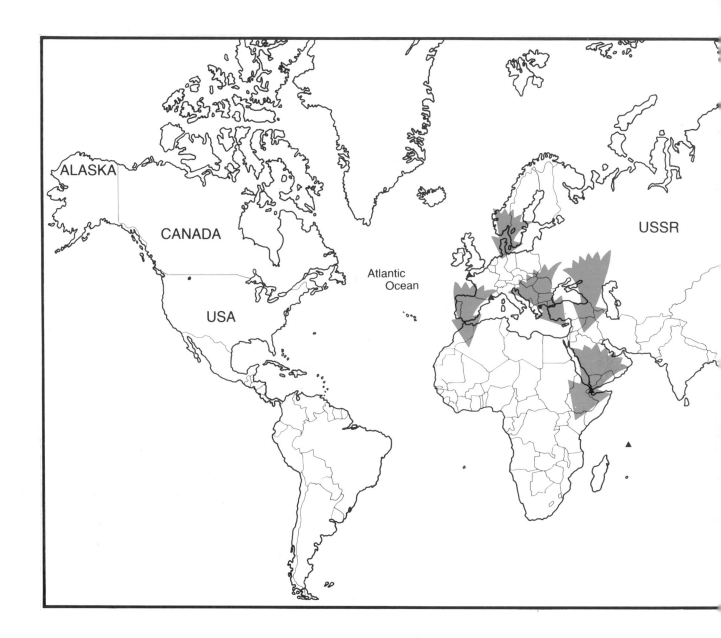

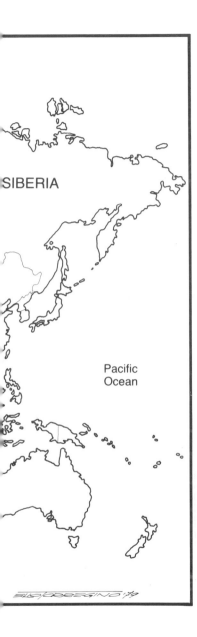

SIBERIA

Pacific
Ocean

Istanbul, thermalling over the domes and minarets before gliding across the narrow waters of the Bosphorus and entering Asia. Quite large numbers of eagles are involved here, especially the reptile-eating Short-toed Eagle and the Lesser Spotted Eagle (*Aquila pomarina*) as well as Booted Eagles and small numbers of some other species.

At the other end of Turkey, birds from western Russia are also travelling south, finding their way along the eastern shores of the Black Sea and then striking inland up the valley of the Coruh river. This particular migration route was not looked at by ornithologists until 1977, when they found over 400,000 birds of prey travelling along it including many eagles, of which Steppe Eagles (*Aquila rapax*) were the commonest. These birds breed on the open grasslands of central Russia and many had the frayed tails of birds which spend long periods sitting on the ground.

But even this huge number was soon eclipsed by the discovery of the next crossing point where both Turkish and

Left: A world map indicating the main annual autumn migratory routes of birds of prey from Europe to Africa. There are also broad-front migrations of birds drifting southward in North America and Asia.

The Steppe Eagle is another long-distance migrant, leaving the frozen lands of central Asia for warmer conditions where prey remains abundant in winter.

The Spotted Eagle
(Aquila clanga) is
another species obliged
to move out of its
northern breeding
grounds in Central
Europe and Russia
during the cold season.
In winter it is most
frequently found in
Ethiopia.

perhaps other streams of birds come together in southern Israel at Eilat. Here over 700,000 broad-winged raptors have been counted in a single autumn.

Eagles are late to leave their summering grounds. Storks, which though quite unrelated have also developed soaring flight and must therefore use the same migration routes, usually pass through Turkey in late August and early September when Honey Buzzards are also on the move. Next comes the main wave of Common Buzzards while the eagles bring up the rear in late September and October. So by carefully timing your visit to

Istanbul or Eilat you can be fairly sure of seeing these birds, often at very close range as they come low over the hilltops before spiralling up to glide on south towards Africa.

The return migration in spring is much less spectacular. Numbers are smaller then because winter mortality has taken its toll. What we see is the coming year's breeding population, heading back to their traditional haunts.

Similar migration pathways exist in other parts of the world, where birds follow the line of a mountain range or, for instance, funnel down the isthmus of Panama en route from North to South America.

Counting the numbers of birds on passage in these places is not just a matter of fun. It gives us an annual check on the fates of eagles and other species. That tells us about changes in their environment and may be a valuable way of detecting problems affecting many kinds of wildlife.

The future of eagles is far from secure. With their need for large hunting ranges and abundant prey, human use of land can have disastrous effects. They suffer from pollution, especially the use of persistent toxic chemicals in agriculture, which still continues in much of the Third World. They are still deliberately killed even where they are rigorously protected by law as they are in the United Kingdom and the U.S.A.

Without doubt, eagles need our concern and protection. Only through support for conservation are they likely to survive. But given our help in protecting their habitats and preventing their persecution, they need fear little. They can go for long periods without food, to sit out storms or make long migrations. They can fly through high winds when all other birds are grounded. They may live for many years, perhaps even as long as a human. With our help and tolerance they can remain masters of their world.

Living in the remote coastland of north-east Asia, Steller's Sea Eagle is perhaps one of the most magnificent of all birds. But despite their skill as hunters and their mastery of flight, many of the world's eagles are today endangered.

Index